THE NINETY-THIRD NAME OF GOD

THE NINETY-THIRD NAME OF GOD

poems

Anya Krugovoy Silver

LOUISIANA STATE UNIVERSITY PRESS

BATON ROUGE

PUBLISHED BY LOUISIANA STATE UNIVERSITY PRESS
Copyright © 2010 by Anya Krugovoy Silver
All rights reserved
Manufactured in the United States of America
LSU Press Paperback Original
First printing

DESIGNER: Michelle A. Neustrom
TYPEFACES: Chaparral Pro, text; Stymie BT, display
PRINTER AND BINDER: McNaughton & Gunn, Inc.

LIBRARY OF CONGRESS
CATALOGING-IN-PUBLICATION DATA

Silver, Anya Krugovoy, 1968–
   The ninety-third name of God : poems / Anya Krugovoy
Silver.
      p. cm.
   ISBN 978-0-8071-3690-4 (pbk. : alk. paper)
   I. Title.
   PS3619.I5465N56 2011
   811'.6—dc22
                                                    2010002509

To Andrew

My beloved is mine, and I am his.

—SONG OF SOLOMON 2:16

Then the Lord answered Job out of the whirlwind. . . .
"Have the gates of death been revealed to you, or have you
seen the gates of deep darkness? Have you comprehended
the expanse of the earth? Declare, if you know all this."

—JOB 38: 1, 17–18

CONTENTS

III

ACKNOWLEDGMENTS

I wish to thank the editors of the following journals, in which a number of these poems appeared, sometimes in different form and under a different title: *America:* "Canticle of the Washing Machine"; *Anglican Theological Review:* "Good Friday" and "Christmas Eve"; *Bellevue Literary Review:* "Ode on Porcelain"; *Christian Century:* "Biopsy"; *Christianity and Literature:* "Ash Wednesday"; *Crab Orchard Review:* "At Skyline Caverns," "The Ninety-Third Name of God," "French Toast," and "Blush"; *Healing Muse:* "After a Mastectomy" and "I Hope My Nurses Remember Playing Records"; *Image:* "Lent: Deformed Pussy Willow," "Persimmon," "Late Wake for a Lost Child," "Marrying Outside the Faith," "The Name of God," and "The Burned Butterfly"; *Louisville Review:* "Rapture"; *Many Mountains Moving:* "Mary" and "Lessons and Carols"; *New Ohio Review:* "Letter to Myself, in Remission, from Myself, Terminal"; *Prairie Schooner:* "Remembering 'Dover Beach,' Block Island"; *Southern Poetry Review:* "Maria" ("Mary"); *Vineyards:* "Laying On of Hands"; *Witness:* "When My Father Told Me Stories."

Several of these poems were published in a limited-edition chapbook entitled *Saints of Autumn* (Macon, Ga.: Redbone Chapbooks, 2006), edited by Kevin Cantwell.

The second section of this book is in memory of those women who have died of inflammatory breast cancer, especially Deborah, Juliet, Susan, Angie, Julie, Akiko, Terri, Janice, and Bev. These poems are also in memory of my mother-in-law, Linda Silver.

Many people read and helped shape this book. Much gratitude to Margaret Gibson, Kevin Cantwell, Gordon Johnston, and Kelly Cherry for their generous and honest criticism, encouragement, and kindness. Thank you also to the poets and friends in my writers' group—Sara Hughes, Jacob DeLange, Aaron Zaritzky, and Tanya Melville—for reading early drafts of many of the poems in this book.

I would like to acknowledge my deep gratitude to the Louisiana State University Press for their belief in my work, particularly to John Easterly and to Catherine L. Kadair.

Thank you to Alexandra Rozenman for allowing me to use her beautiful painting as my cover art.

For the title "The Ninety-Third Name of God" I am indebted to my yoga teacher, Molly Martin, whose meditations with light are the source of the poem. The phrase "sip light through my eyelids" is hers.

To my parents, George and Christel Krugovoy, and my sister Claudia, my love.

My son, Noah, gave me reason to fight and to be grateful. I love you.

This book is for Andrew.

THE NINETY-THIRD NAME OF GOD

Canticle of the Washing Machine

Be praised, my Lord,
for the washing machine,
whose swingle flails the soiled and stained.

For he ministers to the splot, the blotch, the spattered cuff.

Be praised, my Lord,
for your spirit that comes upon him,
for his jump and whirl and *jug jug jug.*

(My infant son slept on his shaking back.
The meek love him and cling to his sides.)

For the flange, which shakes the floorboards,
sends the cat beneath the bed.

Be praised, my Lord, for the agitator,
through whose pivot and plunge into tub
many of the most smudged are cleaned.

Be praised, my Lord, for the delicate cycle,
in which lace and wool can eddy.

Blessed is the soapy breath
that sweetens each room of my house.

Praise and bless the Lord, whose will is done by these God's servants:

wringer, pulley, drum.

I

Is there anything more important
than hunger and happiness?
—MARY OLIVER, "WRITING POEMS"

The Poem in My Childhood

The poem was the wood and the way out of the wood, the dog I summoned
     with my tears, my father's proof for the efficacy of prayer.

My mother wove a ribbon of poetry into my braids, looped them
     around my ears as doorways for images.

When I looked for a muse, a frog climbed the steps of my house.

The voice of crickets, cicadas, wind, and the several voices of winter.

Poetry grew right up to the porch of our rented house. My grandmother
     sent wolves to chase me home in dreams.

In church, the poem, male and female, stood half with my father
     and half with my mother.

When I tried to sit, an old woman pulled the chair out beneath me.
     Later, when I took the Eucharist, she pressed candy into my hands.

My father played chess, my mother rubbed honey into the joints of her fingers,
     my sister and I floated face up in the mountain's green shadow.

The poem was a glass I filled with light sipped through my eyelids.

A woman had planted her garden with pinwheels. She served us potato soup
     and peaches from her tree.

We were *greedy girls,* to pluck those whirling silver flowers.
     Can't you see she's poor?

Shopping bags of empty bottles turned into coins in my hands.

I met a girl who controlled spring and summer. Her favorite ice cream was strawberry.
     When I laughed at her, she made it rain.

I was afraid at my grandmother's funeral to lean down and kiss her face.
The poem growing inside me shriveled. It had grown fat on my grandmother's
      butter and icons.

In the picked-thru cornfields, cawing the secret names of rot and apples, ravens alit.
      The poem was tangled in the seeds of a pumpkin like Sleeping Beauty's suitors.

At school, I suffered from mysterious aches. The poem hid in my pocket.
      The teacher accused me of daydreams and stealing pencils.
When the sidewalk broke open my forehead, a butterfly healed me.

The poem was the book my father took down from the shelf before I could read,
      the engraving of a girl beneath silver firs.

The poem kissed me on both cheeks like a *matushka*. It draped a stole over my head
      and heard my confession.

Fireflies

The photographer has caught them in a tent of netting,
the darkness above and behind defined by a dome of streaks and sparks.

I never harmed them, growing up. To me, they were traces of magic
in the ordinary dusk, like the beauty you find in the surprised faces

of girls, or in the gold coins that tumble from saints' open mouths.
Long Augusts, my sister and I chased them up and down the lawn,

catching as many as we could on our thin bare arms, or tracing
the flight of a single flare into the trees, brighter than snowflakes

and floating not down, but up. I see fewer and fewer every year,
the same poison that kills mosquitoes killing the fireflies, too,

though my mother swears, two summers ago, the backyard lit up
like a skyscape, all that brilliant mating borne on the summer's swells.

When I think of fireflies, I remember the June my husband and I,
in our first house, danced evenings to Johnny Mercer's "Glow worm,"

singing *Light a path below, above, and lead us on to love!* how I swished
my skirt around my thighs, while the empty rooms gleamed around us.

Blush

It's much better to be thirty-four than fourteen,
to speak, now, without the blood pooling in my cheeks,

the skin stained pink like fingers seeding pomegranates,
the lack of control over veins' hot flush and flame.

Then the waiting, waiting for the blood to calm and sink
the way the parachutes we shook in gym class ballooned

before falling, gently, back to flatness.
Eventually, my face recovered its paleness,

people stopped staring or joking, and boys wouldn't think
I liked them with a word as simple as "hello."

Longing hasn't stopped since then, or breathlessness,
or the pause that comes from looking at a stranger's lovely face.

But at least I've hushed my body's murmurs. I've wet
my fingers and stilled the heat of that smoking wick;

I've left you, my blush, my teller of truth and lies,
my unlocked diary of vessels and tissue, my burning sister.

To the Word "Girl"

Because you shimmer like the milky gold skin
of honey unspooled onto a slice of bread;

because, like quick birds swirling steeples,
you're stitched of dark, light, sound;

because, distilled, you'd take on summer smells:
lip gloss, doughnut shop, salt and water;

because you make the crisp swooshing sound
of vintage skirts ballooned and swaying on a rack;

because in college I disowned you as demeaning,
confusing you with the helpless and trite;

because *woman* drags its second syllable behind it
like a book's final volume, like a married name:

when someone calls me *girl*, my body arches
and lightens, the threads that root me unravel,

and I recall myself, fifteen, splitting open pods
of milkweed, that sudden release of silk and breath.

Mary

There's a Mary for everything:
for limestone, for subways, for birches.
There's a Mary for college football,
for the homeless, for abandoned cats
and dogs, for sneaker factories and suburbs.
Everywhere, she casts pitying
eyes over cathedrals and gardens,
rear-view mirrors and asphalt highways.
And in one small village in Austria,
Maria von dem Schnee, heaped with candles
and evergreen boughs, blesses the snow,
blesses the skiers, the boot makers, the cows
in their stalls, stomping and breathing white
plumes through the soundless, snowy evenings.
When, in my narrow bed, sleep won't come,
I think of Maria's placid face, her small hands
folded, her perpetual benedictions of frosted-
over car windows and frozen locks,
and my own heart, frigid in its socket
the day I told my lover that I wanted to leave,
our bedsheets and our hands chapped with cold.
She was my own Mary then, she knew my thoughts
like a mother, she whispered *Be still, my daughter*
and covered me in her easy snow, blessing
my winter, its deep and early shadows,
the ice beneath my eyelids and the good, good sleep.

Hunger

Ten years old, nothing
in the fridge
but a jar of green olives,
soy sauce, packet
of yeast.
Downstairs, *Sesame Street.*
Upstairs, your mother
locked in the bathroom,
water running,
and your stomach gnawing
like a lawn mower.
Whimper into the cat's
complacent fur,
chant with the purple Count,
one, two, three . . .
The world, it seems,
has refused you,
has sealed itself
against you,
stoic as an uncle.

> <

The cat wakes to life
at the screen door.
Late spring,
the season of jasmine
and skinks
on the porch.
He's caught one,
long and slender
as a finger,
hybrid of twigs
and sea glass,
tiny ribs
raised

like the veins
of new leaves.

> <

You could pry
open the jaws,
save a life,
but the cat's hunger
is too quick.
And besides,
somebody is touching,
for the first time,
the hollow space between
your breasts,
the moaning
you hear coming
not from the cat
but from your own
strange
and silken
mouth.

Marrying Outside the Faith

Choosing you, I forfeited my wedding crown, the thrice-
circled altar, the Slavic hymns that rise and fall at Vespers

like stippled swallow's wings. For you, I lost the red
and liquid breath of God inside my throat. Seasons turn

differently, not marked by the altar's changing silks,
the wooden body of Christ carried at Lent from the cross.

The kisses of forgiveness, weekly bows of lip to icon
or sudden crook to knee. Thumb and finger's cruciform.

For me, you forfeited the splintered wedding glass and children
born into the faith with smearing of placental blood.

Choosing me, you gave up the shofar's moan at new moon's turn,
pockets emptied into water, the sukkah's fruited beams,

the Hebrew prayers your great-grandfather the cantor died chanting,
God's name bound around his wrists. Kaddish's stoop and bend.

When curtains draw, we'll learn to move by touch and sound:
by the flame that cowls the mantel's candle, the crackle of leaves

crushed at the dimmed path's edge. We'll share bread between our teeth.
In certain Russian icons, a sheet of silver sheaths the painted wood.

But always, the artist cuts holes over Christ's face and hands,
releasing from metal those dark oval eyes, the human fingers' faithful kiss.

II

And all my sour-sweet days
I will lament and love.
—GEORGE HERBERT, "BITTER-SWEET"

Biopsy

Each time that we have some pain to go through, we can say
to ourselves quite truly that it is the universe, the order and
beauty of the world, and the obedience of creation to God that
are entering our body. After that how can we fail to bless with
tenderest gratitude the Love that sends us this gift?
    —SIMONE WEIL

The pathology report an icon; the tissue
staining the slide, God's kaleidoscope.
And those cells, obeying their DNA,
cosmic dust as they whirl and split.
Why not praise cancer, relentless, blind,
that seeks and finds the lymph and blood?
Because I am unthankful, rude.
Because if I accept this gift,
I will change, I will vanish from the earth.
In Russia, an icon of Mary has wept
for twenty years. Mary, do you see
my nuclei mutating, like words
in *whisper down the lane*? This same God
took your son away. Help me disobey.

Blessing for My Left Breast

Your skin slit round with a scalpel:
be brave.
Rise to the aluminum tray, the biopsy needle.
Go, nipple; go, milk ducts; go, veins.
Take with you my lymph nodes,
canaries of illness, blood cells' puff balls.

Blessed be my chest wall for surrendering.

Now you will never shrink and wrinkle with age,
clove-studded orange, bittersweet.

Taken in your beauty, let the last hands
that hold you
be gentle.

Persimmon

I place you by my window so your skin can receive the setting sun,
so your flesh will yield to succulence, lush with juice,
so the saints of autumn will bless your flaming fruit.

Because cancer has left me tired.

Because when I visit God's houses, I enter and leave alone.
Not even in the melting beeswax and swinging musk of incense
has God visited me, not when I've bowed or kneeled or sung.

Because I have found God, instead, when I've crouched in bathrooms,
lain back for the burning of my skin, covered my face and cursed.

Persimmon: votive candle at the icon of my kitchen window,
your four-petaled stem the eye of God in the Temple's dome,
tabernacle of pulp and seed,
dwelling place for my wandering prayers,

I am learning from you how to praise.

Because when your body bruises and softens, you are perfected.
Because your soul, persimmon, is sugar.

Good Friday

This day, the faithful will not speak, in prayer with Christ.
It's been years since I've seen the wooden body
lifted from the cross, the altar draped in black and stripped
of blooms. Still, I long for intercession, for that God
most merciful, long-suffering and of great goodness.
In a dream, a faceless angel commanded, *Obey the law.*
I argued, and he paused, amended: *Obey the spirit of the law.*
Sitting here, I imagine my prayers burning in the sweet smoke
of beeswax. I bow toward the IV that empties drop by drop.
Remember me, Oh Lord, in thy kingdom. The nurses murmur, *Rain.*
Before the white curtains, let a priest read my name.

Lent

Deformed Pussy Willow

Not the branches

we cut each

windy March

to hang with eggs

dyed red.

Not those

we bless

with palms

& smoke.

These arced

spines & split

limbs bud

through straining

bark. Backs

humped & bent,

bound. *Does*

God suffer

these husked

velvet knobs?

Stunted,

a wreath

of tumors.

Yes, He does.

Gather them

for procession,

for the table

& icon,

crown for

weeping Theotokos.

The Name of God

Like a baker, swaddling the juice and heft of apples in pastry,
I want my mouth to cradle the delicious name of God.

Kissing the Torah, I breathe the dust that has lain on the name of God,
imagine ink on my indrawn breath.

I will dream myself into the body of a bee. I will enter the honeycomb
and sip the scent of blackberry in the golden name of God.

I will open the windows of my house so the name of God can write itself
on my walls with pigment of breeze and pollen, with stylus tipped in light.

If my heart were an amber room, I would inscribe the name of God
over its doorways, and once a year I would flame it down to spicy smoke and oil.

When I was a girl, I drank from the chalice and felt the wine's heat travel
down my bones, each pressed grape's drop alit with the secret name of God.

And later, full of grief, I let a woman press hard against my spine and felt
life rushing again through my body, releasing the clenched-up name of God.

I want the name of God to frost over my sight, to loop the tides to my ears.
How can I be frightened with those vowels in my lungs,

flaring like paper lanterns?

To My Body

Open yourself to me.

You have suffered great losses.
Hands have breached your thresholds.
You have delivered the dead
and the living. You have bled.
Your glands, linings, fat,
have been raked
and exhumed. Body—poisoned, cut, burned—
too tired to rise, you've risen.

How easily I used to slip from my wet bathing suits,
leaving slick skins on the bathroom floor.

Even now, oh body, I will not
believe the evidence, the stitched
flesh and puckered flap.

Our time together is short.
Do not leave me.

After a Mastectomy

I want to be whole,

to uncup, again, a breast's blooming
chrysanthemum.

Or, failing that—

       be true, restrain—

imagine a man's mouth wet on what remains.

Lying in Bed

When I rest my scar against your chest
and you touch the place my breast was once,
the skin seamed shut, stitched flat and blue,
I wonder if you miss the flesh
I used to press against your ribs.
This absence pulls my tendons taut;
the ridge of scar dulls touch and kiss.
But through this loss, both new and real,
my heart beats closer to your ear.
Lay it—listen!—against my skin.

I Hope My Nurses Remember Playing Records

I hope my nurses remember playing records,
the way we'd slide from paper slip each disc,
holding it still between our flattened palms,
easing it gently (A side, B side, back and belly),
down to the table. The wrist raised,
needle suspended, the pause to gauge
the proper place. It was important to wait,
to sink the point—don't slip!—into its groove.
Big stick, the nurses say, before the needle
enters muscle, or drains the opened vein.
Sweet ease, funk, crescendo, *oh.* Dancing
late night in a darkened rec room. Furrowed,
rutted, scratched in love and worn from use—
I hope my nurses remember playing records.

All the Others

One of you raises horses. One of you won't stop
talking. One of you has stopped wearing wigs,
your scalp fine as mohair.

In your mouths, the recitations of drugs
could be succulents or semiprecious stones.
Xeloda. Navelbine. Anzemet.

I don't know your names.

I listen to the tapping of the nurse's gloved fingers
on your wrists. The sluggish blood won't rise.
The needle keeps insisting: open, open.

Sleeping side by side, we forget
as our IVs drip their silent ablutions. We wake.
We complain about the heat.

One of you won't stop talking.
We feel safe. The way I once felt safe in the lunch room, junior high,
one of you to the left and the right. Our friendship bracelets

and crinkled paper bags. Our fists smashing the table in unison,
We Will We Will Rock You. One day we all wore sailor's blouses
and knickers. Hanging upside down on the jungle gym,

my braids brushed the ground. I held hands with my best friend.
We looked down at the sky. We told each other

we'd live a long, long time.

Lamentation

O Lord, forgive the words I hurl against you.
Do not despise me for the wrath I bear you.
But be merciful to me; my hope is wan and slumbering.
Heal me, oh Lord, for my body has risen up against me.
My breast, my breast has petrified.
My soul shrinks, a womb after stillbirth.
Lord, how long?

Hearken, O Lord, save my life; save the lives of my sisters.
None of these dead can sing of your mercy:
Linda, Terri, Juliet, Janice.
How can their sealed mouths praise you?

Wailing has exhausted me;
every night, while my husband sleeps, I weep beside him.
No cloth can absorb my tears.

My lungs choke on this night, my Lord;
my throat grows hoarse with the names
  of those who have perished.

Blot out the bees exulting in my bloodstream.

For you, my Lord, will not forget
  my weeping.
Surely, you have heard my petitions.
Surely, you will save us
  who suffer.

Letter to Myself, in Remission, from Myself, Terminal

You'll come to hate your own poems,
read them as pretty wisps of wishful thinking,
all those images just a splash of colored oil
sloshed over a pool gone rancid. Admit it.
Atheists always scared you. And no wonder.
Those nights you switched on the fan so no one
could hear you scream into your pillow, weeping
and biting your own hands like a motherless
monkey, banded to a body that despised you,
a suit of coals with a jammed shut zipper.
Instead of the truth, you took refuge in stories
and souls, wore the word *survivor* like a pink nimbus.
All the while, my dear, I waited, knowing
you'd catch up to me one day. I'm holding the black-
backed mirror to your face. Look into it.

Black Friday

Your box can't hold this weight, the mailman says,
then puts the catalogs into my hands.
All these pages to skim and corners to crease:
how quickly time gets lost beneath the task.
And then within the stack, I find the book,
her last; her hair in the photo curled as it grew back.
She's one month dead and I've survived, so far,
to pass the morning making lists. *Forgive me,*
I want to say, *for the way my life betrays your death:*
for the smallness of my hours, the forgetfulness
that lets me live, for this spending I have left
to do before the season's candles burn down
one by one, in the wreath that marks the briefest
advent of the sun.

In memory of Deborah Tall

Everything Is Perfect

If my cancer recurs,
if I vomit from chemo,

help me follow the one who knew
she was dying, who turned
to the man wiping clean her face

and said, *Everything is perfect.*

Scrape me like a nutmeg, Lord.
Release my fragrance.

In memory of Akiko

Ode on Porcelain

Shining surfaces are easily scratched.
To clean, use a sponge, plenty
of warm water, and the powder
called Bon Ami. Wipe top
to bottom, starting with the tank,
its gurgles the music you slept to.
The lid is next. Take care to scrape
splashes from underneath (wear gloves)
with a brush set aside for this purpose.
Then lift the seat, the one she trained you
to lower at night without a crash,
and scour the scum, mold, and caked-
on vomit from her last days at home.
Mildew thrives beneath the rim;
if neglected, it multiplies black and blue.

The bowl's a birdless sky—
so many times it took your gaze.
Remember that you made her visits here
more bearable by rubbing her back,
by holding her up in her weakness.
Now that she's dead, this too will be your task.
You will clean the toilet, kneeling,
every week. This surface remorseless.
This polish surrendered to grief.
And then, one day, the rust will enter.
Welcome it into the fissures.

Ash Wednesday

How comforting, the smudge on each forehead:
I'm not to be singled out after all.
From dust you came. To dust you will return.
My mastectomy, a *memento mori,*
prosthesis smooth as a polished skull.
I like the solidity of this prayer,
the ointment thumbed into my forehead,
my knees pressing hard on the velvet rail.
If God won't give me His body to clutch,
I'll grind this soot in my skin instead.
If I can't hold the flame that burned my breast,
I'll char my brow; I'll blacken my pores; I'll flaunt
with ash this flaw in His creation.

This Afternoon

The dark half of the year has come at last.
The dead will leave their mounds to seek
the tables where their children eat; their graves
will flame with candles; and my son will don
his mask and fill his bag with strangers' treats.

What sweetness, this remission, this afternoon
of painting, with my boy, a face to frighten
vengeful ghosts. For our drop cloth,
Obits from Sunday's *Times*. Sitting here, I
pretend that I'm too young to number

with these dead, though one's a man my age:
just thirty-eight. Like me, he had one son.
It's luck that I've survived, or grace, or genes.
We've daubed his face with orange streaks.
He wouldn't mind, I think, our bristles on his smile:

his name another wick to light,
these early dusks, these lengthening nights.

The Burned Butterfly

> Thus this restless little butterfly of the
> memory has its wings burned now and
> cannot fly.
> —TERESA OF AVILA

Char my wings. Lord, singe
these cells of forewing, hindwing.
Blacken memory's sky blue
shimmer, its thousands of cells—
each startling pigment, each
dorsal and ventral venation—
the coppered glint of flight,
Oh Lord. If prayer is forgetting,
let the colored dust of decades
rise in air, let me put away
all fluttered moments trapped
within my hair. These bodies
of memory—crippled, drab—
across the thirsty earth do blow
I bring You, Lord, the rest
of it: my driving mind,
my flightless soul.

A Little Order and Beauty

Oh order, oh beauty, accept me today as a communicant.
Let me eat at your table. Burn your spices in my house.

I will chant your Prokeimenon of honey and warm breath,
of a bed in a quiet room and shadows on the ceiling,

the sparrow's feet curled around the swaying lilac twig,
the peas my son lines up in rows those dinners when he's sleepy.

Because maple seeds will always pinwheel to earth,
because astronomers have mapped the lengthening sky,

if sickness returns to me, whittling my muscle from bone,
I will look for you everywhere, I will dictate the evidence.

In plotted graph and pigment's smudge, I will see
through the spaces into you. I will see you in the spaces.

At Skyline Caverns

Water has hollowed, like a well, the room
        through which a stream still flows,
dissolving the weak and softer rock. We walk
        beneath the limestone vaults.

An ache in the earth has traced these pathways.
        Loss made possible the river in which
the white trout swim. Its blind surface shivers
        as our guide throws fish food in.

"An erosional landscape," he says, switching shut
        the lights above our heads. Hushed
in the dark, unable to mark the shapes around us
        with our sight, we can hear the water

that corrodes and builds. And in the final chambers,
        what tourists come down here to see:
the white stone flowers that grow, no one knows how,
        in high and buried spaces. From these

scarred roofs, bone blossoms hang like brittle stars.
        Drip by drip they radiate. One inch in seven
thousand years, they grow each tear by chalky tear, as if
        the air draws milk from these bare walls.

We pause beneath their shimmering weight. If I could,
        I'd pluck them like a bridal spray, a bouquet
of lacquered shells. I'd press to my breastbone the luster
        of the cleft and damaged earth.

Laying On of Hands

i

The congregation's small,
so we take turns.
My hands press firm
on someone's crown
as though my warmth,
this moth-wing health,
could pause the hum
of spinning mind,
or bind the fraying body.

ii

Shaken to tears by a stranger's back,
bent thin beneath his moss-green plaid,
Grace flowing not *out* (too proud,
imagining myself God's pipe and syringe)
but *up* into my palms, these needy hands.
Why can't I stop crying? A woman murmurs—
The scan I had last week was bad.
Her shoulder blades, her pearled spine.

iii

Not through oil does Christ heal,
but through the aged, obese,
those requiring help to stand or kneel,
through all of us who crave the grease
and spice of unction smeared on skin,
these offered hands, these bodies leaning,
bent, and cresting toward (against) God's will.
Speaking wick and chaliced breath:
Grant us, Lord, our life and health.

Nothing

> What would I trade to regain
> my life the way it was?
> The word is *everything*.
>   —MAXINE KUMIN, "GRAND CANYON"

Looking at photographs from three years ago,
I see that woman I was, her smile
the stupid, thankless smile of the lucky.
A cloth has been dropped between our faces.
My body's coastline, convulsed and reconfigured,
bears its single breast, its twin now frozen or burned.
And yet, when I lower myself into the bath
and receive from my husband's hands the naked body
of our infant son, the curve of his back nestling
against my belly, his head against my scar,
I remember the crescent of skull I saw emerging
between my legs, its damp promise of life.
Sitting in the tub, my toes turning water off, then on,
what would I trade for the life I live now?

The word is *nothing*.

III

The rabbis taught: It is not permitted for a person to enjoy anything
of this world without a benediction, and whoever partakes of this world
without offering a benediction has committed an act of sacrilege.
—THE TALMUD, 35aa–35b

When My Father Told Me Stories

I sealed myself off like a round of dough,
let his words whistle through me like steam.

I refused his father's disappearance, the subsequent
fires (they kept no records), the Great Hunger's
starving children on Balashovskaya Street.
I refused the charred bodies of his ghosts.
Always an errand to run when he started to talk.

But now there's too much skin on his thinning arms.
His muscles shrink like egg yolk inside a painted shell.
And this man who once shouldered Christ's body
from the cross, then dropped his forehead to the floor
in prayer, listens to the liturgy on shortwave radio.

Time rides on the backs of his hundred pills,
like Baba Yaga in her mortar and pestle, gathering
bones to prop up her hut.

                              So tell me, Papi,
about the drowned and the beaten, the priest-
beekeeper who vanished, abortions in wartime.

And the cage, 1944, you saw hanging, swinging
from its monstrous hook. How the woman inside
crawled toward you, eager, hoping for a rescue.
Of course you couldn't help, how else to survive?

                              Rotten century,
when I poke my fingers behind your panel,
the gnawed-through wires still spark and singe my skin.
Your curses ruin the food on my fork, stick
like pitch to my trembling hands.

But I'm my father's oldest daughter. Who else
will accept these stories now? What unearthed

bells will ring *atone atone*? I offer my memory's
open, blistered mouth: bring me

the dark bread, the fist-
ful of salt.

Wish for a Poet

No one better than a woman with cancer
to pin like a drafting compass at the center
of your poem, her leg braced in a slow dying,
able to turn and turn like the neatest metaphor.
Write her being raped by death, or eaten
bite by bite, illness an octopus latched
between her thighs. Use her for any social disorder.
What better sign of pollution than her failing
bowels, how better to snigger at vanity
than the once-beautiful face with its flaps
of skin, and the horror of her made-up eyes?
She offers you her blood counts, tumor markers,
her collapsed veins and hollowed bones.
And, should she die of this disease, you may divide
her up among your manuscripts. Her corruption
will suffice for any number of arguments.

Late Wake for a Lost Child

You had no body by which I could set candles.
I was hollow as a jack-o'-lantern, my insides scraped and flushed.
I'm planning your wake now, after you've been gone for half a year,
because on the radio I heard the last guitar work of a murdered man,
his voice still living though his bones have disappeared,
because a girl riding past me on a bicycle caught the wind
in her blouse, which billowed out to hold the invisible.
I'll invite to your wake the unbroken ball of dandelion spores,
the clock's face gleaming 11:11, whatever else I wish upon.
As scenery, October's extravagant buckling, its blazonry of loss.
But how will I recognize you?
The gaps in the maple, the light startled to find such spaces.

Lessons and Carols

Christmas Eve, my mother and sister and I stand
in the darkened church, making ourselves a tight row,
and each year, I find myself unable to sing
the words that we always save for this night.

It's not just the dead who leave their silent
footfalls on the stone, or the living faces around me
growing older and silvered, year after year falling away
like buttons from their sleeves.

It might be the other things we've lost:
the deep snows I remember from my childhood
in winters now strangely warm and wet,
the paper windows we opened one by one,
peering into their milky secret worlds.

Or it might just be the notes that linger and drift in the candle-
gilded air on this winter night that celebrates life and birth,
the notes carrying us through the cold air and the earth
to the dark breast of the mother, reminding us of sleep,
of calm, of everything we desire and lose and hope to recover
that's peaceful, and tender, and mild.

Christmas Eve

The tree is waiting. A night bird sings.
Hush buries the streets.

At church, the roof drew candlelight into its beams.
A son slept against his father's chest, flame rounding his cheeks.

At one time, God built a body to contain himself.

The icicle shines with the light that melts it.

I prayed for a child.
My body built him, feet to heart to sucking mouth.

Darkly rocked the waters.

The tree is waiting. Light defines its branches.

Fetal Heartbeat

The doctor finds it: a heartbeat's rapid flutter,
like the wings of millions of monarchs returned
again for the winter to the mountains of Mexico,
branch after branch awhir and rustling with butterflies'

long migration and rest. They've traveled hundreds
of miles after breeding, these black-and-rust Valentines,
these milkweed-fed tiger lilies of the Gulf Stream,
folding and unfolding their wings' powdered hinges.

And beneath the rolled seam of my skirt, the heart
pulses of a child, almost a child, I wasn't sure I could carry,
a wild corded bit of skin, teeth, and fists, waiting,
waiting, starting to turn, not belonging to me, but mine.

I don't know how far it traveled, or from where. Oh,
I wanted it abstractly, imagined opening myself to life
the way a glazier fits frames with panes of glass, letting
in light. But I couldn't envision these filaments catching.

Now, like a deaf woman given, for the first time,
hearing, I listen:
every cricket, every peony's slow cracking, every monarch
wing's and lash's flitter, every scrape of pen on paper, magnified.

The Thin Place

I've been there.
I've touched that membrane,
blown on it, stretched it
into a bubble
with my breath.
It caught my reflection,
shivered,
and almost, *almost*
detached.

But something drew me back,

the way my son,
emerging wet-skulled
through the almond-shaped
entryway,
paused,
then pulled back
into the tethered warmth
of the only place
he'd known.

Jellyfish

How much better, I think,
        to have taken the form of a bell

and been able, in darkness,
        to knell my own frail blue light.

(Another dead.) To follow
        the swells so placidly, without fear.

To let life run right through my body.
        (And she a mother. Photographing

her daughter among purple lupines.)
        To swim through my luminous poison.

And not, like I do, to thrash, choke,
        kick at the news. (Another dead.)

Or, at each bone's ache, grab at life
        and feel my clasp slip through it,

untouchable tissue. Body, chalice,
        I'd like to turn transparent and float:

tide-drawn moon, blooming skirt,
        eyeless dancer ascending and dropping.

(You, who broke the surface so soon.)
        Found at last, lashed with such ribbons.

In memory of Julie

A Handful of Berakhot

For lifting a child from his crib
Blessed art thou, O Lord, Our God, Ruler of the universe,
whose speech is difficult to translate, who wakes us with Your waking.

For cracking open an egg
Blessed art thou, O Lord, Our God, Ruler of the universe,
who breaks open the golden gates of the ark.

For buckling my son's shoes
Blessed art thou, O Lord, Our God, Ruler of the universe,
for the tongue and the sole, for binding his foot to the earth.

For slipping my prosthetic breast into my bra
Blessed art thou, O Lord, Our God, Ruler of the universe,
who raises the dome from its ashes.

For reading the obituaries
Blessed art thou, O Lord, Our God, Ruler of the universe,
for these haiku tied, a single day, to foam, to sun-lit branches.

For a brain scan
Blessed art thou, O Lord, Our God, Ruler of the universe,
for whom matter is translucent as aspic.

For waiting
Blessed art thou, O Lord, Our God, Ruler of the universe,
who knows how eternity terrifies.

For laughing
Blessed art thou, O Lord, Our God, Ruler of the universe,
for our breath that returns to You in the wink, the pun, the double entendre.

For hearing of a friend's remission
Blessed art thou, O Lord, Our God, Ruler of the universe,
for stilling the teeth of these hungry beetles.

For viewing a fetus on a sonogram
Blessed art thou, O Lord, Our God, Ruler of the universe,
for this flickering glimpse of a soul in transit.

For riding the ferris wheel
Blessed art thou, O Lord, Our God, Ruler of the universe,
whose eye surveys the carnival, whose seats (sing, hymns) circle round,
        swing up and down.

For going to the post office
Blessed art thou, O Lord, Our God, Ruler of the universe,
for this purgatory of letters, for the scales and stamps; for Your thousand many-
        keyed boxes.

For writing a geometric proof
Blessed art thou, O Lord, Our God, Ruler of the universe,
whose laws we can only begin to deduce when we start (*I am*) with the given.

For seeing a Himalayan poppy in a gardening catalog
Blessed art thou, O Lord, Our God, Ruler of the universe,
whose language, in exile, surprises: the petals of a poppy not red, but blue.

For walking along a boardwalk
Blessed art thou, O Lord, Our God, Ruler of the universe,
who provides a path along the tides, who sweetens our mouths with custard.

For driving in fog
Blessed art thou, O Lord, Our God, Ruler of the universe,
for the chiaroscuro of fogged-in lampposts, for landmarks transfigured and strange.

For writing a poem
Blessed art thou, O Lord, Our God, Ruler of the universe,
for this crown-piercing squall of blossoms.

For a wedding anniversary
Blessed art thou, O Lord, Our God, Ruler of the universe,
whose faithfulness is played out in these knotted, dreaming bodies.

For admiring a full moon
Blessed art thou, O Lord, Our God, Ruler of the universe,
who, beneath the darkening bow of trees, shakes a dress of light onto my body.

Sugar

I swore it, *no sugar,*
and for a year, I kept my word,
but at his first taste of ice cream,
oh, the greedy hands pulling
the dish toward him, his frantic tongue
tweeting like a chickadee, little
marauder, and soon it was cookies
glazed in milk and sugar, one in each fist,
crumbs finding each furrow of corduroy,
Hansel in pajamas marking trails
from room to room; and me, mother
in thrall to my child, folding eggs
into batter as he walks his palms
across the countertops searching for more,
as he points to the moon and cries
Cookie! And he tastes it, and it is.

Rapture

When the world ends in abrupt glaring light,
people lifted unexpectedly out of their shoes
like startled babies hoisted by their armpits,
whole buildings—elementary schools,
banks, public libraries—will empty,
as suddenly vacant as miniature
Christmas villages, their pastel façades
hollow behind storefronts and porches.

A sudden relinquishment of sport coats
and diapers, pantyhose trapped limply
in the branches of trees after floating
in unforeseen winds, the *thump*
thump of helmets hitting the sidewalk
from the tops of telephone poles,
the repairmen's bodies gone.

The dresses: wedding gowns prickly
with beads and buttons, abandoned at altars
like the heroines of old romance novels,
tulle veils stunned puffs of marshmallow.
All the prom dresses, their ruffles, ruching,
slick taffeta shiny as 7-Up, and white
wisps of communion dresses drifting
innocent as milkweed.

I think of all the clothes I've worn,
decade by decade unraveling like a seam:
the matching skirts my sister and I
wore for Russian dances, velour soft
as a cat's back, pastel crocheted caps
in which I watched as men pierced
heaven to walk over the moon's pocked face.

All over America, millions of pairs
of jeans grow slack, while obis,

dirndls, chadors, and saris collapse,
faces and bodies unwrapped like chocolates
shedding their tinsely foil wrappers.

And yet, what a waste, all those precisely
stitched darts and tucks, fitted to the body,
the seam that nestles the small of the back,
that rides up the calf and the thigh, cradles
the heavy breast in its cup of lace and wire.
Gold lame of the drag queen, an old man's
last suit, grown larger on his shrinking body,
cardigans passed like lollipops from sister to sister.

And so I wonder, will some wayward angel,
still loving the mess and tawdriness of life,
find her way to a deserted department store,
wander unbothered through now quiet aisles,
the Muzak silenced, merchandise in heaps,
zip herself into a dress as smoky as a glass
of scotch, a dress she would have worn
on a late, late night, and stand before the mirror
as the silk pours like caramel over what
once were her hips, whether she will love
the caress of the cover, the flawed and gaudy flesh.

Public Displays of Affection

Today, the International Lovers Organization for Voluntary
Expression (LOVE) rallies in Calcutta, husbands and wives
modestly lip to lip for love under placards: "A Kiss for Peace."
I want more. Want the hand beneath my jacket, the tilted head,
a kiss as flagrant as white pumps on Ash Wednesday.

Come here. It's still daylight. Still time to lean over the table
and kiss me slowly, like in the movies, as though I were passing
some sweet thick liquor, anise, into your mouth.

French Toast

Pain perdu: lost bread. Thick slices sunk in milk,
fringed with crisp lace of browned egg and scattered sugar.
Like spongiest challah, dipped in foaming cream
and frothy egg, richness drenching every yeasted
crevice and bubble, that's how sodden with luck
I felt when we fell in love. Now, at forty,
I remember that "lost bread" means bread that's gone
stale, leftover heels and crusts, too dry for simple
jam and butter. Still, week-old bread makes the best
French toast, soaks up milk as greedily as I turn
toward you under goose down after ten years
of marriage, craving, still, that sweet white immersion.

Remembering "Dover Beach," Block Island

I never understood the *grating, long withdrawing roar*
until I closed my eyes and sat beneath the bluffs
of this rocky, shingled shore, listening to the waves
as they slide, ringing, back into the sea. So easy now
to hear through Arnold's lines the pebbles lashed and tossed,
the melancholy bells of rocks worn oblong in the tides.
Pressed against my cheek, stones retain the coldness of the deep.
We'd come for a wedding: witnessed vows, danced beneath
a tent, and then took flight to bed. This morning, climbing
past hedges gone over to red and fleshy hips, past feathered
goldenrod, then down to these deserted cliffs,
I remember that great poem, and how we, too,
have been flung about by chance, or God, and stripped by loss,
and how you've brought me joy, and love, and light, and help
for pain, and how we stand on this shore together and let
the water cool our naked feet again.

The Ninety-Third Name of God

Ya Noor (O Light)

If I can breathe light into my nostrils,
if breath can open my crown so that light
pours downward and then outward, light
drenching the brain and puddling
in my sockets, light running down my throat
straight into the cavity of my chest
and then spreading, a light-slick, light flurry,
cracker snap, torrent of loosed light
rushing through ventricles, winding through colon,
light seeping into the slub of liver and stomach,
threading through ribs and pooling in the pelvis
and then, through the blood and lymph, causing muscles
to shimmer from within, and the skeleton, too,
a dancing lantern, a lattice filled with fireflies,
light in the joints, the long and heavy bones, light
forming sparkling runnels in the toes; and if the light
didn't remain in the body, but instead, depending
again on the breath, flared through the skin and
dispersed into a fog, a mist encasing the whole light-
soaked body, what then of my body could be said
to be separate from this light? And if the light
were related to the light of stars (which it must be),
as well as to the light of the sun, then what of me
would not be star-cloud, star-stream? If I could immerse
myself in the ninety-third name of God, I would fear
no longer tumor or death. I would drink light,
I would rinse my hair in light, I would rub my shoulders
with its grains and seeds, I would anoint myself in lunar
oil, I would make love with every wide-open, glowing,
humming luminous cell of my body pulsing and aflame.

NOTES

"The Poem in My Childhood": The word "matushka" means "little mother" and is an honorific applied to the wife of a Russian Orthodox priest.

"A Little Order and Beauty": The title is taken from Czeslaw Milosz's poem, "My Faithful Mother Tongue."

"A Handful of Berakhot": "Berakhot" is the Hebrew word for "blessing."